POWERGLAZED

Laura Shenton

POWERGLAZED

Laura Shenton

Iridescent Toad Publishing

Iridescent Toad Publishing.

©Laura Shenton 2023
All rights reserved.

Laura Shenton asserts the moral right to be identified as the author of this work.

No part of this publication may be reproduced, stored or transmitted in any form or by any means, electronic, mechanical, photocopying, recording, scanning, or otherwise without written permission from the publisher. It is illegal to copy this book, post it to a website, or distribute it by any other means without permission.

All cover images used under a commercial license.

First edition. ISBN 978-1-913779-93-1

The world's changed quite a bit recently
Hasn't it?

Might stick the kettle on
Might not
Dunno

What do you reckon?
What's the damage?

BOOM!

There goes the microwave

A viral video
Telling people
To fry their steak
In a toaster

Yeah mate
Great idea
A dead cert way
To start a fire

Digital watch
Analogue watch

It's all time in the end

Within these pages
Are words at stages
All around
Something something

For more information
Consult our catalogue

Probably going to come back
As a fly one day

It wasn't the plan
But what can you do?

Shut that door!

SLAM-A-RAM-A-DING-DONG

Please yerself then

Spaghetti and chips
Spaghetti and chips

Some gritty bloke
With a finger on the button

Some dark shadow
In a grey belly button

Touch the ceiling
Get the feeling

Shit yer pants
Just frightened ants

Snake in the grass
Oh, what a farce

I'm not going anywhere
Without a satnav

Shouldn't have to

Don't know where I'm going
Anyway

That little dot on the wall
Is it spying
On me?

That obvious dot in your home
Is it spying
On you?

Oh shit!

We broke the fourth wall

A million beeps
Of a news theme tune

Brace yerself
It's worrying time

Hardly ever use it
But fuck, I need it

Keep your receipt
Else you ain't getting no refund

Ever

I'm afraid that's not in stock

Next door might have one

Don't ask me

Fizzy drink
Rotting yer teeth

Addictive food
Robbing yer mood

Cherries and berries
Large Cornwall ferries

Big pills
Small pills

Let's fix
Your ills

My time
Your time

Stay awake
It's fine

Documentary
In your house

Busy mind
Of weaving louse

Plastic bags of the past
Paper bags, can they last?

Dumping shit in the sea
Food for you, food for me

Needling me
Needling me

Used to this
Diddle-dee

Everyday
Every day

Oh, butterfly
Where do you be off to?

Hey, wait for me
Please may I come too?

A spike
A poke
A wiggle
And a joke

I must
Admit
I'm dancing
As a bloke

Scrawling poetry
Amateur philosophy

Fidgeting, grumping
Brain is rooted like a tree

Scared of everything
What will be the death of me?

Boba
Sugar tea

Sipping
Not so healthily

Always write yer poems
When you're on yer period

Even sans womb

Not the best time
To turn the light on

Live in darkness
Live in hope

We sure do get a great many channels
On this here TV

I think the licence
Must be due
Soon

Bubblegum
Suck my thumb

You're fucking cute
You online fruit

Cheesy chips for stoners
Crunching next to loners

Shish kebab for everyone
Robin Hood and Little John

That beloved
Childhood TV show

Embedded with adverts
How did we not know?

Great British banter
Great British wit

Are you fucking sure?
Some brains be like shit

(For maximum daftness
See upper-class twit)

Moans about making
A classic trifle

Makes the blummin' thing anyway

Everyone enjoys it
That's a win

The average place
May stink of B.O.

Do online shopping
You don't have to go

Work from work
Work from home

The great outdoors?
Oh, bloody oh no!

The finest ingredients
And most meticulous labour

The food sits in the warehouse
The quality paler

One day
Artificial intelligence
Will be able
To do your washing for you

Probably

You'll have to work for it though

What's in today's paper?
A fuck load of ink

What were you expecting?
And what did you think?

Great British Labradors

Nah mate...

Great British blabradors
Oh, and flabradors

Makeup artist
To the stars

Send that rocket
Up to Mars

Wank around
In fancy cars

Think you're hot shit?
Blah, blah, blahs

They're queuing up
For a drink, you know

It must be special
Well, they should know

People get bored of everything
People get bored of everyone

A new thing arrives
And oh, how they strive
To be the first
To be the worst
To be the anything
To be the everything

Send me an email
Next week will do
Not Tuesday, or Wednesday
Cheers to you

Clean bed sheets
Humble treats

Oh, to be a cat of luxury!

Busy mind
You may find
Peace one day

Please let me know

Instant weight loss
Eighties trend

Will expectation
Ever end?

The shopping centre
Has a lift
Through windows
You may find a gift

Wander around
See how you get on
Such neon crap
To muse upon

That family's going
On holiday

Stole your seats
Stole your hotel
Stole your deckchair
Stole your ice-cream

So many apps
In your palm
In your lap

Immediate doing
Quick thinking on tap

Jumbo tub of jam
Massive chunk of ham

Post my food on the internet
And show how big I am

Even channel-hoppers
Can't escape
Reality TV

Admit it
You've seen it
Haven't you?

Can't afford it
But I'll buy it anyway

Thought for the numbers
Can come back another day

In some ways the humans changed
In some ways they didn't

Did the dogs change?
Did the cats change?
It's hard to tell
But it's still doubtful

Global warning
On the cusp of fear

Please don't stop loving me
Lend me your ear

Ain't nothing gonna happen
'Til I've charged my phone

Can't lose this connection
Else I'll be alone

God forbid
A millennial
Eats avocado
On toast

Stereotype danger
Fuck, that was close

Autotune anything
Airbrush anything

It's still art

Just keep making it

Something something
Postmodern
Something-or-other
Conclusion thingy

www.ingramcontent.com/pod-product-compliance
Lightning Source LLC
Chambersburg PA
CBHW041150110526
44590CB00027B/4181